Praise for *Drive Your Career*

"*Drive Your Career* provides you with actionable steps to take charge of your own career and accelerate your professional growth. In a world of constant change, where careers take on many shapes and forms, having a resource like this gives you the practical tools needed to navigate your way to success. It's the perfect book for anyone who takes their career planning seriously. In fact, I wish I had it at the start of my own career!"

Tracy Burns, chief executive officer of Northeast Human Resources Association and co-founder of Hytched

"Ed Evarts is a master at transforming a complex problem into something so much simpler. Every day I embrace his words of wisdom. 'It's the hand you've been dealt, Joe, what do you want to do—fold, bluff, or take action?' And try 'the power of pause.' *Drive Your Career* is filled with ideas that really work!"

Joe Callahan, president and chief executive officer of Cabot Risk Strategies

"*Drive Your Career* is a great way to explore how to be more of a leader in your own career. Often, we don't take the time and steps to ensure we are following a pathway that helps us. In my work with Ed Evarts, we have touched on a number of these ideas and I would recommend them all. Even if you only read a few of them, your likelihood of making progress in your career development is significantly enhanced."

Bob Castellucci, founder and president of Partnership to Prosperity

"*Drive Your Career* puts decades of industry-leading career coaching and client experiences in your back pocket. This is a go-to guide for anyone looking to start their career on the right path or shake up their career if things are not going as planned. I've read a number of complex books on leadership and career development—Ed Evarts is clear, colorful, and gets right to the point."

Mark Conley, vice president of finance at Kaleido Biosciences

"*Drive Your Career* instantly puts you in the driver's seat of your career progression and shows you how to put the pedal down to move forward. Ed Evarts's thoughts and ideas are fantastic and this book will put you on a direct path to success. Whether you're just starting out or are a seasoned professional, these ideas can help us all."

William Crooker, chief financial officer, executive vice president, and treasurer of STAG Industrial

"*Drive Your Career* is a pragmatic and useful guide to anyone looking to improve their working environment. I particularly like the 'be part of the solution' approach and taking charge of one's destiny. A sure recipe for success in anyone's career, regardless of their role or position."

Harry Ebbighausen, former North American president of Iron Mountain

"Ed Evarts provides succinct advice from his diverse career, much of which can be applied with great success regardless of role, title, or scenario. Being a highly curious person myself, I particularly enjoyed the chapter on curiosity which had some terrific tips on how to ask great questions while navigating the potential political pitfalls too many companies have. I believe there is something for everyone in this book."

Bill Flynn, coach, speaker, and bestselling author of *Further, Faster*

"In this time of uncertainty and change, taking responsibility for your own success is more important than ever. Skillfully navigating interpersonal challenges is the prerequisite for progress on the professional path. Ed Evarts has expertly mapped out this terrain. Drawing on decades of real-world coaching wisdom, *Drive Your Career* blends stories, insights, and tools into a guide that's as enjoyable to read as it is practical to apply."

Alain Hunkins, bestselling author of *Cracking the Leadership Code*

"I thoroughly enjoyed reading Ed Evarts's *Drive Your Career*. The nine 'high-impact ways' are very relatable because of the concrete examples from the real-life case studies at the beginning of each chapter. Whether you're starting out in your career, or are already well established, this book will benefit anyone seeking to make a positive impact."

Jane Kourtis, deputy general counsel of Bright Horizons

"Written in an accessible, anecdotal style, *Drive Your Career* is loaded with practical advice that will resonate with anyone who has ever felt their career get off track."

Brian Madden, co-founder and senior vice president of Lexington Solutions

"There's nothing more frustrating than feeling your career has stalled out, your potential is sitting untapped, and you can't see a way forward. In *Drive Your Career*, Ed Evarts gives you nine precise moves you can make to accelerate your effectiveness and build the career you want. Implementing just one may change your life forever."

Dave McKeown, author of *The Self-Evolved Leader*

"Straight-up, hard-hitting, and practical advice on how to make progress in your career from an experienced coach who is not afraid to put on his 'coach-sultant' hat and give you the facts."

Tom Morin, keynote speaker and bestselling author of *Your Best Work*

"*Drive Your Career* is a terrific examination of real-world situations involving leaders navigating experiences we all encounter day in, day out. Valuable insights in every chapter."

Steven Nelson, chief executive officer of ILPA

"*Drive Your Career* provides clear, actionable career advice in an easily digestible and engaging format. Ed Evarts's use of poignant examples to demonstrate career-driving behaviors provide the context for the invaluable tools that readers can use to make forward progress in their careers. The hardest part might be deciding on the top three behaviors to start with since they are all great!"

Jennifer Reilly, president and chief operating officer of Safety Partners, Inc.

Drive Your Career

Drive Your Career

9 HIGH-IMPACT WAYS TO TAKE RESPONSIBILITY FOR YOUR OWN SUCCESS

ED EVARTS

excellius
PRESS

ISBN 978-1-7345004-0-0 (paperback)
ISBN 978-1-7345004-1-7 (ebook)

Published by Excellius Press
www.excellius.com

Produced by Page Two
www.pagetwo.com

Cover and interior design by Taysia Louie

www.excellius.com

CONTENTS

INTRODUCTION

WHAT CAN I do about my performance issues, Ed?" The question came from one of my leadership coaching clients, a medical director at a large technology company with offices in the Boston area. I'll call him Kevin.

Kevin's question is one I hear a lot, and I mean *a lot*, from the clients I see as a leadership coach. In Kevin's case, his performance issues had to do with his difficulties speaking up at senior-level meetings and his fast work pace, which made it hard for others to be engaged on teams with him and to work with him one on one.

As a coach, my goal is to help clients like Kevin answer their performance questions for themselves. In some cases, though, my clients need more of a "coach-sultant"—a coach who, with the client's permission, can put on the hat of a consultant and answer non-coaching questions directly. Such was the case with Kevin.

"I'd be happy to answer that question," I replied. "First, I need your permission to stop being a coach and start being a consultant. What kind of help do you need right now?"

"I need a consultant!" Kevin quickly exclaimed.

"Okay," I said. "Here are a few ideas that I share with many of my clients. I believe they'll help you too."

Kevin listened intently to what I had to say about the behaviors and actions that I felt would help him, and he left our meeting more energized than I'd seen him for a long time.

I was struck by how excited Kevin was to hear the handful of simple ideas I'd shared, and I began to think about the other advice I frequently offer. Within minutes, a short list emerged of the behaviors and actions that have helped so many of my clients become the drivers of their careers.

I've met a lot of people in my thirty-five-year business career, which has included twelve years as a leadership coach. Some of my clients are drivers and some are passengers. Passengers are along for the ride, not caring where they end up. Drivers care. Drivers have a vision for their career; they take responsibility for their success; and they make purposeful decisions to get from point A to point B.

My goal with this book is to help you become the driver of your career and make positive progress at work.

When I started to tell colleagues that a simple set of behaviors and actions can help *everyone*, many reacted with disbelief. Back when I began working as a coach, I would have agreed with their conclusion. Now that I've been coaching business leaders for over twelve years, though, I've seen firsthand how remarkably consistent my clients'

"My goal with this book is to help you become the driver of your career and **make positive progress at work.**"

needs are. While the specifics of each client's situation are unique to them, at the core of addressing many work-related issues are common behaviors and actions that, if practiced regularly, can help anyone make progress in their organization, earn the respect of their co-workers, and be more productive and happier at work.

When I say *anyone* can benefit from the nine simple ideas in this book, I really do mean it. As you read, you'll see that:

- **The ideas are industry-agnostic.** Whether you are in pharmaceuticals, law, finance, engineering, or any other industry, you can implement these ideas at any time.

- **The ideas are role-agnostic.** Whether you are an entry-level employee, a manager, a director, a vice president, or a president, all of these ideas apply to you.

Here are a few other things to keep in mind as you read:

- **While you may not need to implement all nine ideas, you likely need to apply many of them.** Chances are you already have incredibly busy workdays, and adopting many new behaviors and actions at once may not be possible. That's okay. You can try out a few ideas at a time, or rotate them. As long as you're implementing some of them, you'll be better off in your work experience than you are now.

- **The ideas are not presented in order of importance.** I have no desire to tell you which ideas are more important for you than others. You will be the best judge of what you need to do to be more successful at work. As I say in idea #2, no one knows you better than you do.

* **Doing something recurrently matters more than doing it frequently.** When you start adopting new behaviors and actions, applying them recurrently—that is, at regular intervals—is more important than applying them frequently. Many of my clients initially feel that when it comes to a new behavior, more is better. In truth, more is not better if you can't keep it up.

Sounds simple, right? Well, the reality is that even though these nine ideas *are* simple on the surface, it takes sustained effort and focus to put them into practice. That's why you're reading this book!

Each chapter of this book explores one of the nine ideas. The chapter covers what might be stopping you from implementing the idea, and shares tips that have helped my coaching clients put certain behaviors and actions into regular practice to achieve real results. You can read straight through the book or dip in anywhere to find the inspiration that applies most to you at any moment in your career. Throughout, key phrases that I believe you need to remember are highlighted.

Okay. Are you ready to learn more about the nine ideas that I've shared with most of my clients, most often, to make a difference in their career?

Wait! This sentence reminds me to pause and acknowledge that what I'm about to share with you is *advice* as opposed to *opinion*. An opinion reflects what someone

"Doing something recurrently matters more than doing it frequently."

thinks, regardless of how accurate the basis of their opinion may be, or their interpretation of the facts. My belief on gun control, for example, is an opinion. Advice reflects what someone thinks and has experienced based on the time they have spent in an area of practice and the knowledge they have gained. For example, behaviors that your doctor tells you to follow are advice. Your doctor's recommendations and prescriptions are based on knowledge and experience, not opinion.

Advice is more important than opinion. This book contains advice. The behaviors and actions you will read about are things that many people in organizations around the globe can and should do to improve their work experience. I'm confident that if you try to follow my advice and take responsibility for your own success, you'll improve your work experience too.

Ready to become the driver of your career? Let's get started.

1

HAVE A POSITIVE RELATIONSHIP WITH YOUR BOSS

"**The secret of successful managing** is to keep the five guys who hate you away from the four guys who haven't made up their minds."

Casey Stengel, American Major League Baseball right fielder and manager

RADHANATH IS A successful businessperson who has a terrific relationship with his boss, Ted. Ever since Ted hired him, Radhanath has made impressive progress in the organization, with two promotions and regular generous pay increases. "I don't think you know how brilliant you are," Ted tells Radhanath one day. Radhanath's career prospects seem limitless.

To Radhanath's surprise, everything changes when Ted decides to leave and a new boss, Victor, steps in. Victor is very different from Ted. Victor and Radhanath do not see things eye to eye, the way Ted and Radhanath did in the past. Radhanath's share of interesting projects and high-profile assignments drops off. Victor does not seem to trust Radhanath, nor does he promote him or reward him with generous raises.

During Radhanath's professional demise, one of his direct reports, Donna, develops a strong and great relationship with Victor—so great, in fact, that Victor regularly goes around Radhanath and directly asks Donna to assist with special projects and high-profile initiatives. While it frustrates Radhanath that Donna is constantly pulled into the game while he is left on the sidelines, his poor relationship with Victor makes it difficult for him to broach the situation, let alone resolve it. Radhanath's workload continues to shrink, and within two years of Victor's arrival, Radhanath is laid off. Guess who takes over his role? Donna.

Why has this happened to Radhanath? Did his bad relationship with Victor hurt his career? Would it help if he had connected better with his new boss?

In my experience, the answer is a decided yes. To move ahead in their career, every one of my clients has needed to have a good relationship with the person they work for. Having a positive relationship with your boss is not optional.

Why must you have a positive relationship your boss?

When you have a positive relationship with your boss, many wonderful and career-enhancing things—opportunities, praise, promotions, pay increases—are possible. Your life as an employee is easier, you have more impact, and you're in a stronger position to drive your career forward.

When I think of the benefits of having a positive relationship with your boss, I come up with an acronym that spells the word "help."

H is for harness

A boss with whom you have a positive relationship will help you harness your skills and apply them effectively in your

"Having a positive relationship with your boss **is not optional.**"

———————————————

organization. If your workplace is like most, you're probably working on dozens of things at once and your energy and focus are diffused. A positive relationship with your boss can help you concentrate your energy on the activities that help your organization and your career the most.

E is for evolve

As the saying goes, "Things that don't grow, die." This is especially true in our fast-changing world. Your boss can help ensure that your ideas grow and evolve in ways that benefit your organization and ultimately advance your career.

L is for learn

To move forward in your career, you need to be different tomorrow from how you are today. In many organizations, professional development falls more on the shoulders of individual employees than on the training department. A boss with whom you have a positive relationship can help you learn how to do your job better and be more impactful.

P is for proactive

Few behaviors are more important than being proactive. Organizations will love you if you prepare them for an ever-changing marketplace by always thinking about what's around the corner. A boss with whom you have a positive relationship will remind you to look around the corner. Wonderful bosses will challenge you and discuss what you are thinking.

WHAT ABOUT YOU?

How is your relationship with your boss? If your relationship is poor, can you think of any situations where that has hindered your career? If your relationship is positive, can you think of any situations where that has helped your career?

What is your current relationship with your boss?

When you don't have a positive relationship with your boss, the conflict, distrust, hidden agendas, lack of clarity, and lack of confidence between you can be like a third person in the room whose sole aim is to get in the way of any progress.

Take a few moments to think about your relationship with your boss. Then on a scale of 1 to 6, with 1 being very troubled and 6 being very positive, rate the relationship you have today:

1   2   3   4   5   6

If you rate your relationship on the low end of the scale, you're not alone. In my work as a leadership coach over the past twelve years, I have asked hundreds of clients or prospective clients whether their relationship with their boss could be better. A full 85 percent have said yes. Wow! That's a huge number in my client base alone. A 2015 Gallup survey showed that out of 7,272 US adults, 50 percent left their job to get away from their manager at some point in their career in order to improve their overall life.[1] That's another huge number.

How about you? Whatever your goals are for your career, your relationship with your boss needs to be positive for you to prosper and get ahead in your organization.

What might be jeopardizing your relationship with your boss, and what can you do about it?

Here are some of the most common reasons why your relationship with your boss may not be as good as you'd like, and some tips for overcoming the barriers.

Style
You and your boss may have different leadership styles that consistently create conflict between you.

What can you do about this?
Different styles are very common in the workplace. Schedule time with your boss to talk about your respective styles—what you both like and don't like. The more transparent you both are, the more likely it is that you'll find ways to keep your differences from eroding your overall relationship.

Personality preferences

You and your boss may have different personality preferences—that is, preferred ways of interacting and working with other people—that give rise to frustration and irritation between you.

What can you do about this?

I encourage you and your boss to complete a TypeCoach or Myers-Briggs Type Indicator assessment and review your outcomes together. I guarantee that what you learn about each other's personality preferences will pave the way for a more positive relationship.

Geography

You and your boss may work in different buildings, cities, states—or countries! Even an excellent relationship can suffer if you don't see your boss regularly. You may feel that if your boss doesn't see you enough, they will forget you exist.

What can you do about this?

Don't let geographical distance get in the way of a positive relationship. Make sure you reach out and connect with your boss frequently by phone or email, and by all means, include a visit whenever you're in the same building. Ask your boss how you can deepen your relationship despite the differences in your geography.

Temporary assignment

You may report to a boss on a temporary basis. Unless your boss is deeply focused on building your skill set and the connection between you, the short-term nature of the assignment may delay your progress in building a positive relationship.

What can you do about this?

Treat all colleagues to whom you report, including temporary bosses, in positive and helpful ways. You never know whom you may meet again in the future, and sometimes a temporary boss becomes your regular boss. Don't look back in regret; make your best effort even with a temporary boss.

Matrix environment

In today's complex and fast-paced organizations, many bosses have several areas of responsibility—some that overlap and some that don't. The more varied your boss's tasks, and the more work they have to lead, the less time they'll have to spend with you. This can erode your ability to build a strong relationship.

What can you do about this?

No matter how many areas your boss supervises, make sure you operate as a helper, not a hurter. A helper is someone who your boss feels helps them achieve goals and make positive progress. A hurter is someone who hinders your boss's progress. Always look for ways to be perceived as someone who helps.

Hired vs. inherited status

Bosses are naturally more invested in people they've hired than in those they've inherited. It's the difference between

"I chose you voluntarily" and "you were given to me involuntarily." Your hired vs. inherited status with your boss could have a big impact on your relationship.

What can you do about this?

You can't change whether you were hired or inherited by your boss. Regardless of your status, you need to make sure, as with the previous situation, that your boss sees you as a helper, not a hurter. Being a helper means overcoming how you and your boss came together and doing all you can to help your boss be successful.

Let's call it "enjoyment"

This might be the trickiest situation. You may not enjoy being with your boss and your boss may not enjoy being with you. The reasons for this displeasure may be one or more of my earlier points, or a new factor altogether. Whatever the reason(s), some folks just don't like one another.

What can you do about this?

While it may be hard to fake it when it comes to your regard for your boss, in some cases you need to do just that. Ensure that you've always got your boss's back, that you're positive and future-focused, and that you work in ways that help your boss succeed. Who knows? If you try hard enough, perhaps your boss will get promoted!

What else can you do to improve your relationship with your boss?

If any of the situations above are interfering with your relationship with your boss, you need to take clear action to mitigate them. Here are three more general ideas that will help you get along better with your boss.

Ensure you know your boss's goals and career aspirations

Everyone wants to believe that other people care about them, and you want your boss to think that about you. The best way to demonstrate that you care is to ask about your boss's goals and career aspirations. Tell your boss you're curious about what makes them tick, and listen to what they say. Knowing your boss's goals and aspirations puts you in a better place to help.

Ask your boss the million-dollar question on a regular basis

Ask your boss the million-dollar question: "What are one or two things I could do differently to be more effective?" (I like the word "differently," as it's less controversial than "better" or "worse.") Ask the question regularly—maybe two to four times a year—and listen closely to the answer. The feedback you hear will be meaningful. This question may be the best method to guarantee that you are behaving in ways that meet your boss's expectations.

"What are one or two things I could do differently to **be more effective**?"

Always watch your boss's back

Always update your boss on things they should know about. You don't want your boss to get caught unaware or underinformed. Bosses hate surprises! If you hear something you think your boss should know, find a few minutes to communicate it in person, or call or text with an update.

WHATEVER YOUR RELATIONSHIP is with your boss right now, it can always be better. On your own, or with a colleague who knows you and your boss, identify a few actions you can take to improve your relationship, using the ideas discussed here or some of your own.

Action #1: _____

Action #2: _____

Action #3: _____

What if you are the boss?

You may be thinking, "I am the boss! Why am I even reading this?" If you are the leader in your organization, you need to know that individuals who report to you are working to have a positive relationship *with* you. That is an important effort on their part.

Be open to these behaviors. Recognize employees who take the time to learn your career goals, who ask you the million-dollar question, or who share valuable information with you and demonstrate that they've got your back.

A relationship is a two-way street. Just as your employees need to have a positive relationship with you, you need to have a positive relationship with them. Strong relationships require more than one person.

Employees who have a positive relationship with you are more likely to be engaged and supportive of your ideas and actions. Enjoying a great relationship with your direct reports is a win for you and a win for them—and a win for your organization.

AS HE MOVES forward in his career, Radhanath will manage his relationship with his boss differently. He will schedule time with his boss and will do the following:

- **Ask about his boss's goals and career aspirations.** Let's face it—we love to talk about ourselves, and we don't want to feel alone. By asking about his boss's goals and aspirations, Radhanath will build bridges to a strong relationship.

- **Ask his boss the million-dollar question.** The answers he hears will give Radhanath greater insight into what's important to his boss and the behaviors Radhanath may need to adopt to get ahead.

- **Always watch his boss's back.** Radhanath's boss can't be everywhere nor see and hear everything. Ensuring that his boss is not surprised by something Radhanath already knows is a great way to build a positive relationship.

Idea #1—have a positive relationship with your boss—is all about striving to understand who your boss is and what makes them tick. Why? So that you can help your boss, and yourself, drive progress in your career and in your organization.

WHAT'S NEXT FOR YOU?

Now is the time to ensure you have a positive relationship with your boss. What can you do differently to improve your relationship with your boss—even if your relationship is good? Even strong relationships need maintenance to stay positive.

2

NO ONE KNOWS YOU BETTER THAN YOU DO

"At the end of the day, **you know yourself best.**"

Abigail Johnson, president and CEO, Fidelity Investments

SINCE BEING PROMOTED into a new role at her organization about a year ago, Sara has had a new boss, Kamran. To prepare for Sara's performance appraisal—an annual requirement for all employees— Kamran reaches out to a number of Sara's peers and internal customers for feedback about her.

Kamran receives a lot of positive comments, yet a number of people identify the same area for development: Sara's ability to follow up on open work items. This feedback is consistent with Kamran's own assessment of Sara. While she frequently takes on new work, she often leaves people, including Kamran, wondering about her progress. Perhaps Sara doesn't see how poor follow-up creates drama for her colleagues and even adds to their workload when they have to pursue her for information.

During their performance appraisal conversation, Kamran starts with the positive observations about Sara's work. He then broaches the critical feedback about her ability to follow up.

KAMRAN: Most of the feedback I've received from others about you is good, Sara. Yet I and your colleagues feel you could be more effective in your follow-up. What are your thoughts on that?

SARA: I try really hard to update my colleagues on how I'm doing with the work that's been assigned to me. I'm just so busy! Sometimes it's hard to update everyone all the time.

KAMRAN: I know you're pretty busy, and you're doing a great job at getting your work done on time. Yet giving updates to your internal clients is also important. I'm curious: have you heard this feedback before, either in your last role at this company or at other organizations?

SARA: You know, I have to be honest. This is feedback I've heard my whole life. I got feedback like this from friends in college and from other bosses at other companies. I can even think of friends from high school getting frustrated with my apparent inability to follow up.

KAMRAN: That's interesting. Given that this is feedback you've heard before, why haven't you done something to get better at following up?

SARA: I don't know! You'd think I would have by now!

KAMRAN: No one knows you better than you do, Sara. For years you've known this is a potential area of concern, yet you've done little to improve it. Maybe it's time for you to get motivated and do something about this area of your performance.

Why wouldn't Sara do something to get better at following up over time? Most of my clients ask themselves a similar question during our one-on-one coaching when we talk about areas they've struggled with throughout their careers. Even though the concern is known to them, and is obvious to others, many of my clients have not taken action to improve things.

No one knows your strengths, weaknesses, likes, dislikes, secrets, desires, and (I'll just say it) lies better than you do. No one—not bosses, peers, subordinates, spouses, family members, friends, or neighbors—knows you as well as you know yourself. So why aren't you listening to yourself?

How do you turn self-knowledge into self-awareness?

My observation that no one knows you better than you do doesn't come from years of scientific study. It comes from more than a decade of working one on one with clients. When I ask my clients, "Who knows you best?" what do you think they say? It is always, *always*, the same answer: "I do."

Yet in today's workplace, people are so focused on goals, objectives, projects, and getting to meetings that they don't spend enough time with the person who knows them best— themselves. As a result, few people are actually *aware* of what they know about themselves. When you have low self-awareness, you can't effectively manage your strengths and weaknesses, achieve your goals in the workplace, or drive your career forward.

"No one knows your strengths, weaknesses, likes, dislikes, secrets, desires, and lies **better than you do.**"

To increase your self-awareness, you need to spend time with yourself, thinking about what you should do to make progress and be successful. I like to call this time "thinking with yourself."

I use the word "with" as part of this behavior for a reason. When you think *with* yourself, you should imagine that you're sitting down with yourself and discussing your goals, dreams, desires, and next steps. Some of my clients use a whiteboard to capture their ideas. Others find a colleague they can share their thoughts with. Some keep a notebook and write down ideas as they pop into their head. You are not there to think *about* yourself, as if you're a voyeur of your own life. Thinking *with* yourself is much more creative and action-oriented.

WHAT ABOUT YOU?

Do you have low self-awareness of your strengths and weaknesses and often feel like the proverbial bull in a china shop? Have you spent time thinking with yourself about your natural strengths and weaknesses?

Why is it important to find time to think with yourself?

Spending time thinking with yourself is essential to building self-awareness. High self-awareness about your strengths and weaknesses is a prerequisite for being a career driver and a great leader.

For example, Steve Jobs proved to be a challenging leader because of his apparent low self-awareness. In fact, his leadership style is still a point of debate today, years after his death. On the other hand, Bill Gates, who many would say is an effective leader *and* has high self-awareness, easily talks about his weaknesses and how he addresses them, and he does the same for his strengths. Gates continues to build a legacy he can be proud of.

Thinking with yourself can also help you think and act more strategically for your organization. One of my favorite books on building meaningful, effective strategies is *Good Strategy/Bad Strategy* by Richard Rumelt. Near the end of the book, Rumelt notes:

> In creating strategy, it is often important to take on the viewpoints of others, seeing how the situation looks to a rival or to a customer. Advice to do this is both often given and taken. Yet this advice skips over what is possibly the most useful shift in viewpoint: thinking about your own thinking.[2]

Rumelt believes that individuals and organizations, whether they realize it or not, own proprietary data that no

"High self-awareness about your strengths and weaknesses is a prerequisite for being a **career driver and a great leader.**"

one else owns at a given point in time. These proprietary data are your personal strengths, weaknesses, likes, and dislikes. No one knows you better than you. It is critical to think with yourself so that you can identify your proprietary data and figure out how to use this information to become the driver of your career.

What should you think about when thinking with yourself?

Here are some opening questions to ask when you are thinking with the person who knows you best—yourself:

- How would I describe my strengths at work?
- How would I describe my weaknesses at work?
- What influences my strengths at work?
- What influences my weaknesses at work?
- What can I do to take better advantage of my strengths at work?
- What can I do to positively influence my weaknesses at work?

These questions will start you on a meaningful journey. Once you've answered them, ask yourself more questions as a way of delving into your initial responses. Your goal is to develop higher self-awareness about your strengths, weaknesses, goals, dreams, and next steps so that you can drive your career more purposefully and be more effective in the workplace.

How do you turn high self-awareness into action?

If you have high self-awareness and self-discipline, you may succeed at managing your strengths and weaknesses on your own. You may find some recurring time to ask yourself important questions, write out your responses, create an action plan that outlines your next steps, and implement the actions.

For most of us, however, managing our strengths and weaknesses is a lot harder than scheduling personal reflection time on the calendar. Here are some ways to turn the insights you gain from spending time thinking with yourself into effective action.

Identify your unique motivator

No one will spend time and energy doing anything if they're not motivated to do it. If you want to start thinking with yourself regularly, and acting on what you discover, you need to find your unique motivator. Do not underestimate the importance of this—if you don't find a motivator, you will fail.

I'm not going to list possible motivators, as the list would be endless and might not include the motivator that will work for you. After all, we are all different people. Whether it's a promotion at work, four weeks of vacation, or a huge raise, the motivator you choose needs to be strong enough to keep you practicing your new behavior. I suggest you find a close family member, friend, or colleague and have a conversation with them about your possible motivators. Have that person ask you, "What will motivate you to create and maintain this behavior?"

Then, once you identify your unique motivator, put it into action. If it helps you build the habit of thinking with yourself, stick with it! If it doesn't, meet with your person again and take another shot at it. At some point you'll find the unique motivator that works for you.

Find an accountability partner

The number-one way to make progress on any goal, and I mean *any* goal, is to have an accountability partner. This isn't just anyone. This is a special person who *cares about you making progress as much as you do*. It can be a colleague, a friend, a family member, or someone you just met who shares your objectives.

Regardless of who it is, you need to be very specific with your accountability partner about what you're trying to achieve. How specific? Here are some examples of how to ask an accountability partner for support:

- "I need to speak more slowly at meetings. I get the impression that people have trouble keeping up with me. During our weekly meetings, could you assess how fast I'm talking and give me two minutes of feedback afterward? It would be terrific if you could score me on a scale of 1 to 6, with 1 being too slow and 6 being too fast."

- "I need to get better at being on time, because my late arrivals are causing meetings to start late. After each meeting we attend together, could you assess my time-liness on a scale of 1 to 6, with 1 being on time and 6 being very late? I would appreciate it."

· "My boss has given me feedback that my PowerPoint presentations are so long and detailed that folks are get-ting lost. As I work on upcoming presentations, would you be open to reviewing them for a few minutes and scoring me on a scale of 1 to 6, with 1 being too short and 6 being too long? That would help me a lot."

You can see that you need to be very specific in telling your accountability partner what topic(s) you need help with and exactly how they can support you. That's why I suggest that your partner provide a numerical score, as in the exam-ples above. Sometimes accountability partners say things like "You were terrific!" or "You really handled that well!" While it's always wonderful to get positive feedback, vague statements like these don't tell you how you are doing com-pared to your goals. Asking for a numerical score forces your accountability partner to pay close attention to your area of interest and give you more meaningful feedback. Plus, you have the added goal of improving your score!

Create an accountability team

Another way to ensure that you find meaningful time to think with yourself and manage your strengths and weak-nesses is to create an accountability team. You can ask individual accountability partners within the team to give you quality feedback on specific topics. Having multiple people support you in several areas will help you make even more progress toward your goals.

As your needs evolve, so should your team. Don't be afraid to thank your current partners, let them "retire," and find other people who can help you in new ways.

Hire a coach

Like an accountability partner, a coach is someone who helps you identify goals and then holds you accountable. Unlike an accountability partner, a coach is trained to help. Also, since you pay a coach, they are usually diligent about managing their own behavior and supporting you. There are coaches who have built entire businesses around holding others accountable—that's how important this action is. Check the International Coach Federation website (www.coachfederation.org) for a coach who can help you.

EVER SINCE HER performance appraisal meeting with Kamran, Sara has spent more time thinking with herself and identifying the proprietary data (strengths, weaknesses, likes, and dislikes) that she brings to her role. As a result of this self-reflection, Sara has identified a couple of areas she'd like to work on. In particular, she recognizes that she needs to communicate more frequently with project stake-holders and follow up with them more regularly.

To make progress toward this goal, Sara identifies her unique motivator: she never wants to receive these crit-icisms again. She wants to be a poster child for effective communication and follow-up with peers. Sara arranges for an accountability partner to give her instant feedback when working on a project with her, and she hires a coach to help her adopt new behaviors so that her peers and internal clients will see consistent improvement.

By being more self-aware and taking specific action to address deficiencies, Sara is moving out of the passenger's seat and is becoming the driver of her career.

WHAT'S NEXT FOR YOU?

Work on building your self-awareness of your strengths and weaknesses. With higher self-awareness, you'll be able to actively manage your behavior to maximize your impact. Who wouldn't want that?

3

BE THE MOST CURIOUS PERSON IN THE ROOM

"We keep moving forward, opening new doors, and doing new things, because we're curious and **curiosity keeps leading us down new paths.**"

Walt Disney, entrepreneur, animator, and film producer

KYLE, AN ENTRY-LEVEL associate at a marketing firm, is a clear extrovert. This means, among other things, that he gets his energy from interacting with others. Kyle also hates the sound of silence and loves to be the first to talk. Whether he's in a workshop with people he has never met or in a business meeting with colleagues, when someone asks a question, Kyle always has to answer first.

This behavior is evident the day Kyle attends a strategic planning meeting with his boss and ten co-workers. When the speaker asks the participants a question at one point, Kyle's colleagues stare at the floor and at their notes as they consider their answers. Not Kyle. His hand immediately shoots up in the air.

Kyle's participation encourages others to raise their hands and join in as well, and as the discussion unfolds, Kyle feels pretty proud of himself. Not only did he go first; he also inspired others to speak up.

Yet when the discussion ends, one key fact stands out to Kyle. The answer he gave, when his hand shot up before anyone else could speak, was ill-conceived and—even worse—incorrect. *How can this be?* Kyle asks himself. *Why didn't I have a really good answer? What could I have done differently to make sure I had a better answer?*

The solution to Kyle's problem is simple, yet most of us don't practice it. The solution is not to be the first to speak—it's to be the most curious person in the room.

Why should you be the most curious person in the room?

If you ask questions about the weather forecast before taking a trip, you can plan your trip better. Similarly, when you ask questions before sharing an idea or giving an opinion, your idea or opinion will be better. Asking questions before you speak allows you to learn why someone feels the way they feel, or whether they have a different opinion from yours, or what they know and don't know. Asking questions is the best way to discover more about what others think or know before you share what you think or know.

Let me give you an example. Sheela, a sales manager for an information technology firm, wants to help her company hit its sales numbers, so she decides to make a proposal to her boss, Louise, to approve the hiring of five sales representatives, strategically located across the United States. Sheela believes that better representation across the country will broaden her company's footprint and result in more sales. She spends hours on a beautiful multi-slide PowerPoint presentation. She works with the finance team to

"The solution is not to be the first to speak— it's to be **the most curious person** in the room."

identify which parts of the country are least represented so she that can determine where to place the newly hired employees. She even works out rates of pay compared to sales production estimates to convince her boss that this is an unbelievable opportunity.

At the meeting with Louise, Sheela is about ten minutes into her presentation when her boss stops her. "I wish you had spoken to me before you went to all this trouble," Louise says. "I wish you had asked me some questions. I would have told you that I just recommended to the operating committee that we shift away from a sales rep model and expand our account management team so we can better service our current and future account base. That's a less costly way to address our weak representation in certain parts of the country. If you'd asked about this before putting together this presentation, you would have used our time more effectively."

What Sheela thought would be a winning presentation has turned into a dud.

What could Sheela have done differently to get to a better place? Here's an alternative scenario.

Recognizing that it takes a lot of time and energy to develop a proposal, Sheela could have stopped by Louise's office to ask a couple of questions first. "I want to help the firm hit its aggressive sales targets this year," Sheela might say. "Before I work on new ideas, is there anything I should know?"

"I'm glad you asked," Louise might reply. "Interestingly, I'm going to make a presentation to the operating committee on how we can reduce our dependency on sales reps and expand our account management team so that the account base we have now, and any accounts we get in the future, get better service. That will address the geographic representation problems you're thinking about, only for less money. What do you think?"

"I think it's a terrific idea!" Sheela might respond. "How can I help?" And Louise might say, "Maybe you can help me create the presentation for the operating committee."

This example shows how two different strategies can produce two different outcomes. If Sheela had paused before investing time and energy in what she thought was a brilliant idea—if she had been the most curious person in the room—her efforts, outcomes, and visibility with her boss, and with the operating committee, would have been significantly different and better.

WHAT ABOUT YOU?

Do you think you know most of the answers right away and quickly jump in to share your thoughts and observations? What has been the impact of your behavior?

Why is it so hard to be the most curious person in the room?

Being the most curious person may sound easy. It's not. If being the most curious person in the room were simple, everyone would do it—yet few do. Here are a few reasons why.

Speed

Most clients I work with describe their workplace as busy. You probably describe yourself as "busy, busy, busy!" "Busy," I think, is the most overused word in today's business environment. It comes from organizational cultures that ask folks to do a lot, with very few resources, very quickly. If you are not moving fast, you are not moving fast enough. You may feel that the need for speed reduces your ability to be the most curious person in the room. Who has time for curiosity?

Confidence

We've all heard workshop speakers or teachers say, "There are no dumb questions." Why does anyone have to tell us this? Why are we afraid that others might think our questions are dumb, or that we'll ask a question that everyone else can answer except us? Has anyone ever said at a meeting, "Wow, that was a dumb question!" Of course not. Yet many of us still lack the confidence to ask questions. In the absence of training and practice on how to be curious, you're less likely to have the confidence you need to ask the questions that curiosity requires.

Recognition

If you're like most people, you focus your efforts on areas that earn you positive recognition. In industries where curiosity is applauded—for example, the pharmaceutical industry—people are more likely to be curious. If no one seems to care about curiosity in your industry, or no one is ever recognized for it, it may never occur to you to be the most curious person in the room.

Despite these restraints on curiosity, being the most curious person in the room, and being curious *before* you start your work, will help you gather all (or almost all) of the information you need to make progress.

How can you be the most curious person in the room?

When you are the most curious person in the room, you will come to better conclusions, share better ideas, and help others who have the same questions yet lack your confidence and intent to ask them.

Here are some things you can do to practice being the most curious person, no matter what your situation.

Prepare

One of the best ways to ask good questions (and not share poorly conceived ideas, like Kyle) is to prepare. For example, if you're attending a meeting, think about the meeting's purpose and its expected outcome, and work on some questions in advance. I'm not suggesting hours

"The most curious person in the room will come to better conclusions, **share better ideas**, and help others."

of preparation—you can do this in as little as three to five minutes. Preparation will help you be more confident about asking questions, it will raise your visibility, and it will help others. Preparation is a core behavior for driving your career.

Identify fallback questions

In addition to the questions you come up with when preparing for a specific meeting, workshop, or conference, it's also good to have a few fallback questions. These are impactful questions that fit any interaction, such as:

- What is (are) the risk(s) of doing this project?
- What is (are) the risk(s) of not doing this project?
- What other ideas do you have to make progress in this area?
- Why is the idea you shared the best idea for us to consider?
- Are there simpler ways for us to do this project?

All of these questions will help you and others think about ideas more effectively.

Ask what questions you should ask

Reach out to the presenter and ask if there are any questions that need to be asked. This is a meaningful way to make sure the questions you ask are helpful and valuable.

Pursue next steps

Being the most curious person in the room doesn't mean you stop being curious when you walk out the door. Thoughtful questions lead others not only to think differently but also to consider taking different actions. As the most curious person in the room, you should be the one to capture those actions and to help yourself and others remember what they are. Take notes or ask that the meeting be recorded. Whatever your strategy, do what you can to help everyone at the meeting ensure that the next steps are pursued.

Do you also have to be a strong listener?

When I try to be the most curious person in the room (and I am still practicing!), I also try to be a strong listener. I see these as two equally important parts of an equation that results in career success:

Most Curious Person + Strong Listener = Success

Someone who is curious but a poor listener will never be an effective leader or driver of their career. If you ask a question and don't listen to the answer, you will severely limit the benefits of being curious. Why? Because powerful questions lead to powerful answers, which lead to more powerful questions, which lead to more powerful answers, and so on and so on. I think you get it. As Albert Einstein said, "The important thing is not to stop questioning. Curiosity has its own reason for existing."

AFTER SAYING INCORRECT things more than once, Kyle begins to listen more and ask increasingly thoughtful questions. He begins to realize that the benefits of fully understanding a topic before suggesting an idea or a solution are more important than talking first. Knowing more about a topic before responding makes him feel more impactful and relevant. Now, rather than being known as the guy who always answers first, Kyle is building a reputation for being the most curious and thoughtful person in the room.

WHAT'S NEXT FOR YOU?

Focus your energy on listening more and demonstrating curiosity. Those who wait will participate more effectively than those who go first.

4

BELL CURVES ROCK

Professor: "I'll start off with the bad news: 90 percent of you failed the exam. [Class groans.] I can't have so many students fail, so I'm going to bell-curve the marks. You all know what a bell curve looks like... Ah... actually, you don't. Most of you failed the exam!"

CAROLINE WORKS AS a marketing manager at a global paper and digital records management company. She loves her job, her colleagues, and the company's mission. She generally works on rolling out new records management ideas to clients to help them manage their paper records more effectively.

Two years into her role, Caroline is assigned to lead the marketing portion of Project Eagle, an initiative that capitalizes on recent advancements for managing paper record requests online. She is asked to present a marketing implementation strategy to the leadership team in two months.

Caroline works diligently on the strategy. She consults technologists and business leaders across the company to learn why these advancements are beneficial for their clients, which vehicles the company can use to market the advancements, and how much additional income the company can anticipate receiving.

At the leadership team meeting, Caroline spends twenty minutes delivering her plan. As she is wrapping up, one team member raises her hand and asks, "Caroline, what are the risks of *not* doing this project?"

Caroline is stunned. Not only does she not know the answer, she hasn't even thought about the risks of not doing the project. *Is this a criticism?* she wonders. "I'm not sure, Susan," she sputters. "I'll get you an answer by tomorrow."

Another team leader jumps in. "Caroline, I know you've done a ton of work on this project," he says. "Can you tell us where our competition is with these technological advancements?" Again, Caroline stalls. "That's a great question Carlos. I'll need to do some research on that. I'll get the team an update by your next meeting."

Another team leader raises her hand. "I'm really concerned about the financial estimates you've given to deliver these tools to our client base. What other financial options do we have?" Once again, Caroline is stumped. She never anticipated so many questions that feel like criticisms of her work. Can't her colleagues see all the benefits this new tool will bring to the company and its clients?

What would have helped Caroline, and what can help you, is to realize that life is like a bell curve.

Why is it useful to think of life as a bell curve?

If you do an internet search on the term "bell curve," you'll find millions of results, which just goes to show how pervasive the bell curve is in our daily lives. In almost anything you experience, a few data points will be highly favorable, a few data points will be highly unfavorable, and most data points will fall somewhere in the middle.

The bell curve principle:

"Some will love your idea, some won't like your idea, and some will find your idea satisfactory."

Caroline's presentation is an example of a bell curve. In addition to thinking about the benefits and strengths that her company's technology will provide clients, she should have anticipated the tough questions some folks might have for her. Then she'd have been better prepared to respond to them.

An excessive focus on the positive end of the bell curve is something I see in my coaching. As my clients come up with ideas or actions for becoming more effective in their workplace, most of them focus so much on the potential positive results that they spend little time thinking about possible negative outcomes—and therefore can't handle the negative questions very well. The result is often a delay in their ideas being implemented.

This is where the concept of the bell curve is so useful. You can't predict how others will react to an idea, so when you're getting ready to share one, it helps to know that you will likely encounter three responses: some will love your idea, some won't like your idea, and some will find your idea satisfactory—that is, they won't love it or hate it; they will see it as good enough.

Caroline's experience is common in the business world. You may well spend so much time on the strengths of a new idea that you neglect to ready yourself for challenging questions about your work. Because you're not prepared, you'll have a hard time answering these questions well. When you are underprepared, projects can end up delayed or even stalled.

If you think about the three possible reactions people will have *before* you present your idea, you'll be ready to respond. There are three questions to ask yourself:

- **How will I interact with those who love my idea?** You may need your strongest supporters to help you convince those who hate your idea that there's more to the idea than they are considering.

- **How will I interact with those who feel my idea is satisfactory?** You definitely do not want these colleagues, who neither love nor hate your idea, to become haters. You need to manage your relationships with these people so that they become more lovers than haters.

- **How will I interact with those who hate my idea?** You need to understand why these colleagues don't like your idea so that you can clarify it for them or even consider changing it. Whatever their reason for hating your idea, your goal is to move them from haters to lovers.

Thinking about the bell curve and your answers to these questions *before* you share your thoughts will help you refine your ideas, gain support for them, and ultimately make positive progress for your organization and in your career.

WHAT ABOUT YOU?

Do you focus so much time and effort on selling your idea that you are unprepared when someone pushes back? What has happened to you when you've been unprepared to respond to someone's pushback?

"The bell curve will help you refine your ideas, gain support for them, and ultimately **make positive progress**."

How can you use the bell curve to be more effective?

Generating a question about your proposed idea or action is a great way to anticipate and plan for people's responses. Let's do an exercise to see more clearly how this works.

For your question to be effective, it should do three things:

1. **Stimulate an emotional response.** Your question should trigger answers about how others will *feel* about your idea or action. This is where the "love it" or "hate it" perspectives come into play.

2. **Be as general as possible.** The more general your question is, the better your curve will be—and the better your preparation for the range of responses. If the question is too specific, your bell curve will flatten.

3. **Lead to a range of responses, not just yes or no.** Two answers will not produce a very good bell curve!

Here's an example. The question "What will people think of my presentation today?" is likely to produce a good bell curve for the following reasons:

1. **It will stimulate an emotional response.** The question will trigger answers about how others will feel about your presentation.

2. **It is general.** You're not being too specific in the way you are asking the question.

3. **It is not a yes/no question.** Your participants can respond in a variety of ways.

Here is what the bell curve might look like:

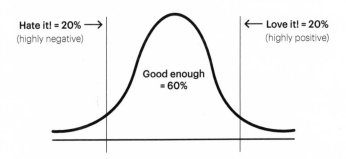

On the other hand, the question "Will my presentation today succeed?" will not generate an effective bell curve. Here's why:

1. **It will not stimulate an emotional response.** The question does not trigger answers about how your presentation will make your colleagues feel. The question is simply about you and your expectations.

2. **It is too specific.** The question is narrow. It's based on a limited interpretation—yours—of what success will mean.

3. **It does not lead to a range of responses.** You will answer either that your presentation will succeed or that it

won't. This yes/no answer will not produce the range of responses you need for a bell curve.

AS CAROLINE REVISITS her presentation, she realizes that before her next meeting she needs to think about all the possible weak spots, options, risks, and impacts of her marketing strategy—in addition to its benefits. She also reaches out to everyone on the leadership team, individually and ahead of the meeting, to assess their thoughts and be even better prepared. By doing her homework this way, and by realizing that just as many people may have concerns about her ideas as may love it, Caroline will be much better equipped for tough questions and criticisms at the next meeting.

This is why the bell curve is so important. Thinking about the full range of people's responses—positive and negative—is one way that career drivers make sure their ideas, their solutions to problems, and their relationships with clients and colleagues move forward. Bell curves rock!

WHAT'S NEXT FOR YOU?

Before presenting an idea, try to consider all the negative reactions your colleagues might have so that you're ready to address them. You are more likely to make progress when you are just as prepared for criticisms as you are for praise.

5

COLLEAGUES ARE YOUR BEST RESOURCE

"Human resources are like natural resources; they're often buried deep. You have to go looking for them; they're not just lying around on the surface."

Ken Robinson, author, speaker, and international advisor on education

TWO WEEKS AFTER being laid off because his employer closed its local office, Kurt finds a new opportunity at a growing financial services company. He is eager to start his new job and is determined to make a great first impression. At his two-day orientation, hosted by the human resources department, he learns about topics such as the history of his new company, how to enroll in the 401(k) program, and how to find the employee cafeteria. Kurt listens intently, asks a few questions, and meets a number of other new employees.

Following his orientation, Kurt spends a couple of days with his new boss, getting briefed on his key areas of work. He finds a training manual in the top drawer of his desk and quickly learns what he needs to do to perform his job well. He works hard and gives it all he can. When his boss occasionally stops by his desk to see how Kurt is doing, Kurt is always positive. When his girlfriend, Nikki, asks him how his new job is going, Kurt says, "Great! Things couldn't be better."

About two months into Kurt's new job, his boss asks to speak with him for a few minutes. As it turns out, his boss is concerned with Kurt's performance. He is so dissatisfied, in fact, that if Kurt doesn't do things very differently over the next few weeks, his job will be in jeopardy.

Kurt is shocked. How did this happen? He thought his new job was going so well. No one, including his boss, has ever told him differently.

That night, at home, Kurt tells Nikki that his situation isn't as wonderful as he thought. Nikki, who has managed employees at a medical services technology company for two years, listens intently as Kurt shares his surprise at his current work status. Then she asks him some questions.

NIKKI: What have you done so far at work to make an impact?

KURT: To be honest, I thought I did a lot of things that would have helped me.

NIKKI: Can you give me a few examples?

KURT: Well, during the two-day orientation, I asked a bunch of questions that I thought were really good.

NIKKI: Do you remember what topics your questions covered?

KURT: Hmm, I think dress code, break times, and employee parking.

NIKKI: Okay. What else have you done?

KURT: I met a bunch of colleagues at the orientation.

NIKKI: Have you stayed in touch with them?

KURT: Not really. I assume they're as busy as I am, learning their new jobs.

NIKKI: Got it. What else have you done?

KURT: I started my work based on what's in the training manual that was left in my desk drawer. That's why I'm confused. I completed every section of the manual. How could I be doing so poorly?

NIKKI: I think I have a few ideas. Are you open to some candid feedback?

KURT: Yes! Please!

NIKKI: Kurt, you've fallen into a trap that any person can get into when they start a new job. I've seen it happen at my office. Every once in a while, a new employee tries so hard to make a strong impression that they dig right in, only to find out later that their boss is unhappy. Their first question is always, "How did this happen?"

KURT: No kidding. That's exactly what I asked first.

NIKKI: Even though you asked terrific questions at orientation, and you met new people, and you used the training manual you found, you didn't spend time on another activity, one that can make all the difference—finding and working with a tenured employee.

KURT: What do you mean, "tenured"?

NIKKI: I mean someone who's been there a while, who's good at their job, and who knows how to help. You know, most new employees are uncomfortable approaching their boss for help. They think they might be a distraction. A tenured employee is a great alternative. They have experienced what you're going through, they can give you insights and direction, and they know the people and situations at your workplace better than you do. If you want to turn things around, ask your boss tomorrow for the name of a colleague who can help you. A tenured employee might be the best investment you can make.

What kind of colleague can be the most helpful?

Organizations are filled with colleagues. They are everywhere! Yet not all colleagues are the same. Some are new to the organization, while others have been there for years, even decades. Some just show up to collect a paycheck, while others are deeply committed to the organization's vision and mission. Some ignore how the organization interacts with customers, while others are very observant of how the organization navigates the marketplace. Some colleagues are collegial; others are not.

To make progress in your organization, the kind of colleague you need to find is what I (and Nikki) call a "tenured colleague"—someone who ticks all of the following boxes:

- **Has at least three to five years of experience in your organization.** Someone who's been on the job for at least three to five years will have experience and knowledge about who and what works well in your workplace, and who and what doesn't. Generally speaking, colleagues who have been at your organization for less than three years won't have the same insight as those who have been around the block a few times.

- **Is seen as a strong performer.** A colleague who is highly valued and visible in your organization will have compelling observations. Your goal is to find someone who is seen as a high performer in their current role and is considered a leader.

- **Knows how to help.** I've saved the trickiest characteristic for last. A tenured colleague is an individual who can help not only because they have experience in your organization and are seen as a strong performer, but also because they know *how* to help. If an employee has not been trained to work with colleagues or is not energized by doing so, it will be a waste of your time to try to tap into their experience.

WHAT ABOUT YOU?

Are you so focused on your own role and your own deliverables that the idea of reaching out to a colleague hasn't even cross your mind? Have you ever thought of connecting this way?

"To make progress in your organization, the kind of colleague you need to find is what I call a **'tenured colleague.'**"

How can a tenured colleague help you?

In her article "Why Are Long-Term Employees Important?"[3] Grace Ferguson points out some of the benefits to employers when long-term (that is, tenured) employees help new recruits learn the ropes:

> Each time you hire a new employee, you must train him. Long-term employees have already undergone this process and can be an invaluable support system to new employees. For example, the same accounting or clerical issue that the new hire struggles with can be immediately solved by a long-term employee, freeing up more time for everyone. If the new employee becomes stressed or overwhelmed by his job duties, the long-term employee can reassure him that in time he will get the hang of it.

Besides being valuable to you when you're new to the organization, tenured colleagues can help you in several strategic ways throughout your career:

- **They know what ideas have (and haven't) worked in the past.** Oftentimes, you may think your ideas are original to your organization. A tenured colleague can tell you how ideas like yours previously played out, which will help you manage your time and energy. They also know when ideas are likely to connect in your organization and industry and when they're likely to be ignored or rejected.

- **They know other colleagues who can help you be successful.** Why spend your valuable time connecting with colleagues who either can't or won't help you make progress in your career? Folks who have been around for a longer time know more about how your organization and industry work. They can connect you with the people who will help you succeed.

- **They will challenge you to think differently about your work.** The biggest advantage of working with a tenured colleague is their ability to use their years of successful experience to help you make faster, smarter progress. Every employee needs someone who can positively challenge their work to ensure it's the best work possible. Even the most successful mountain climber needs a guide to help them find the optimal route. Thinking about your work differently is why you're seeking out a tenured colleague in the first place.

Why are colleagues such an underused resource, and what can you do about it?

Kurt's failure to connect with tenured colleagues is not unusual. The vast majority of my clients, when sharing with me how they are trying to make positive progress in their workplace, do not include the step of reaching out to a tenured colleague.

There are a number of reasons why people, whether new to their organization or not, fail to see their colleagues as

"Every employee needs someone who can positively challenge their work to ensure it's **the best work possible.**"

resources for their own progression. Before I share my clients' reasons, let's start with your own (assuming, that is, that you haven't reached out to your colleagues this way). In the space below, list some of the reasons why you haven't turned to a tenured colleague for help.

_____

_____

_____

_____

_____

Now, here are some of the reasons my clients have given. Should any of these barriers resonate with you, you'll find tips for overcoming them and connecting with the people who can help you drive your career.

Time

If there's any asset people feel they have too little of, it's time. "I didn't reach out to anyone because I couldn't find the time" and "I wish I had the time!" are common responses when I ask my clients if they've turned to a colleague for help.

What can you do about this?

I call this the _Grey's Anatomy_ syndrome. No matter how busy your day may be, if _Grey's Anatomy_ is your favorite show, you'll always find time to watch it. If you can find the time to watch television, you can find the time to connect with a tenured colleague.

Intimidation

New employees are often intimidated by longer-term employees and may feel embarrassed to ask them for help. "Would she even help me if she could?" and "Is he too busy to help?" are common questions my clients consider when they think about connecting with tenured colleagues.

What can you do about this?

Some of us learned a valuable lesson as far back as kindergarten: you'll never know the answer unless you ask the question. If you ask a tenured colleague for help, the worst answer you will get is no. Perhaps your tenured colleague is too busy to help. Or perhaps your colleague would love to help. You'll never know unless you ask.

Clarity

Many employees are unclear about what they most need help with. They ask themselves, "Where do I start?" or "How do I make sure I'm using my colleague's time well?" Because of their uncertainty, they may never ask for help at all.

What can you do about this?

To know what you need help with, you have to spend time with the person who knows you the best—yourself (see idea #2). Find a few moments over the next day or two to start thinking about areas where you need help, and write your thoughts down. Even if the list is not perfect, it's a great place to start.

Knowledge of who's who

Your goal is to find a colleague with at least three to five years of experience, who is seen as a strong performer, and who knows how to help you. That can be tough to do. Most of my clients don't even know where to start, even though finding this colleague may be critical to their success.

What can you do about this?

You actually have a lot of options. You can ask someone in human resources to help identify an ideal candidate. If you have more than one person in mind, you can interview your picks to see who would be the best fit. Also, many organizations have mentorship programs that assign new employees to tenured ones—maybe your organization does too.

Ego

Many of my clients have an active ego. That's not a criticism—sometimes it takes an active ego to succeed in today's fast-paced workplaces. Yet ego may lead these folks to convince themselves that they don't need help. "I can do this myself," they may think, or "I don't need anyone else to be successful." These folks overrely on themselves and undervalue the help of others.

What can you do about this?

Use your active ego to your advantage. Think of how tenured colleagues could help you become even more successful or help you drive your career even faster than you could on your own. My clients with active egos repeatedly talk about how their work experience improves any time they reach out to a tenured colleague.

Company culture

The culture of some organizations may not support connecting with tenured colleagues, or may even discourage it. "I asked for the names of colleagues I could reach out to and no one got back to me," one client told me. "My boss said he couldn't think of anyone who could help me," said another. These are experiences you'll relate to if this activity is not supported by your organization.

What can you do about this?

I often tell clients that they should find out whether collegial support or mentorship is part of an organization's culture during the job interview. Learning this before you join an organization may help you decide if this is where you want to work in the first place. If you've already joined an organization whose culture does not support mentorship, break the trend. Connecting with tenured colleagues is so important that you have to find a way to make it happen.

Who might be your most valuable tenured colleague?

Now is the time for you to reach out to tenured colleagues for assistance. Think about people in your organization who might have the three characteristics we covered earlier, and list them here.

Tenured colleague's name	Has at least three to five years of service Who has "been there, done that" at your organization and knows its history?	Is seen as a strong performer Who is repeatedly promoted, is seen as influential, and is highly praised by other colleagues?	Knows how to help Who is trained in or energized by working with others? (You can interview people to assess their fit.)

THE MORNING AFTER his conversation with Nikki, Kurt finds the courage to follow up with his boss. He asks if his boss can identify a strong performer who can work with Kurt to improve his performance. Kurt's boss loves the idea and asks one of Kurt's colleagues, Stephanie, if she can help Kurt acclimate to his job and the organization. Stephanie is excited and happy to help, and she and Kurt begin to collaborate immediately.

Stephanie's first step? She shows Kurt that the most recent training manual is online!

WHAT'S NEXT FOR YOU?

Reach out to tenured colleagues in your organization in order to make progress. There are others around you who have experienced what you're experiencing today.

6

PLAY
THE HAND
YOU'RE
DEALT

"Life is not always a matter of holding good cards, but sometimes, **playing a poor hand well**."

Jack London, novelist, journalist, and social activist

TOMAS IS ABOUT a year into a new job in a fast-growing engineering firm, and no day is like another. Some days Tomas loves his job; other days his job frustrates him. When he talks about his workplace with close colleagues and friends, he finds that most of them have similarly mixed feelings. Those who are new to their organization say their workplace is not exactly as they *believed* it would be when they were interviewed, and those who have been in their position a few years feel their workplace is not exactly as it *should* be.

As he navigates his way through the company, Tomas learns that the issues facing the firm and the personalities populating it are more complicated than he initially thought—or in some ways was led to believe. It's not that the people he met in the interview process were lying or denying the reality of their workplace. It's just that some of them don't see the things Tomas sees. Others see the problems as normal. "Everyone experiences issues at work. Get over it!" is their view.

As Tomas enters his third year on the job, his boss announces that Tomas is being considered for a promotion. While this should be great news, Tomas has doubts. His concerns about the company's culture have only increased with time, and he wonders if he should turn down the promotion or even find a new place to work. He has already invested two full years of his life at this company. Can he just walk away?

Tomas's situation reminds me of what many of my clients experience in their workplace. In an effort to help them understand their situation better, I often tell my clients this: "Whether you want it or deserve it, your workplace is a lot like a poker hand. Whether it's a good or bad hand, it's the hand you've been dealt."

How is your workplace like a poker hand?

In January 1998, I decided to begin a biweekly poker game and invited six of my best friends to play. To my pleasant surprise, they were all interested—or, as we say in poker, they were "all in." Over twenty years later, we're still playing. We've learned a lot about poker, about other playing styles, and about winning and losing.

During one game, as I was dealt good and bad hands, it struck me that a workplace is a lot like a poker hand. I started to use this analogy in my coaching work with clients who found their workplaces more stressed, disorganized, or unfocused than they thought they should or could be. "Whether you're dealt a good hand or a bad hand," I found

"Whether you want it or deserve it, your workplace is a lot like a poker hand. Whether it's a good or bad hand, **it's the hand you've been dealt**."

myself saying again and again, "it's the hand you've been dealt."

As we'll see later, you have three options—fold, bluff, or take action—no matter your situation. First, though, let me explain why a poker hand is such a useful analogy for navigating your workplace.

Why does it help to think of your workplace as a poker hand?

As I work to become an accomplished coach, I've adopted the practice of relating an experience that a client finds stressful to an experience that's typically less so in order to help the client understand the stressful situation more clearly.

This is where my poker analogy comes in. When I compare my clients' workplace to a poker hand and suggest they have only three options—fold, bluff, or take action to make things better—my clients seem better able to understand their situation and, more importantly, to think clearly about what to do about it. "Oh my, I'm bluffing!" a client will say. "No wonder I'm so frustrated. How can I take action to make things better?"

Now we're getting somewhere.

What type of hand are you holding at your workplace?

When you interview for a new job, or are considered for a promotion in your current workplace, it's highly likely that you'll be led to believe that the situation you're stepping into is better than it really is. After all, the folks interviewing you have a position to fill, so they will typically exaggerate the positives and diminish the negatives. That's human nature. You may hear things like "We're not perfect" or "A few things could be better," yet it's highly unlikely anyone will tell you how things truly are, especially if the workplace is really bad. Similarly, if you've been at your organization a few years, there may be a gap between your actual workplace situation and what you think it should be. Most of my clients experience gaps like this.

Since life is like a bell curve (see idea #4), your work situation—whether you're new to the job or many years into your career—will fall into one of three categories:

1. **Your situation is better than you thought it would be.** Every once in a while, one of my clients will say their workplace is fantastic. If that's the case for you, excellent!

2. **Your situation is worse than you thought it would be.** Maybe your workplace was made to feel like heaven but has begun to take on hellish characteristics.

3. **Your situation is good enough.** This is the apex of the bell curve, and this is the feeling that most of my clients experience—that no workplace is perfect.

Only you can assess if you're holding a good hand, a bad hand, or a so-so hand when it comes to your workplace. What you *do* with that hand depends on where you want to go. As we'll see, no matter what you do—whether you fold, bluff, or take action—it's the act of *doing* something, rather than passively holding the hand you've been dealt, that will help you become a driver of your career.

WHAT ABOUT YOU?

Have you been dealt a good or a bad hand when it comes to your workplace culture? If you've been dealt a bad hand, are you thinking about folding or are you investing in bluffing? How tiring is each of these behaviors?

How can you play your workplace hand to make positive progress in your career?

If you decide that your workplace situation is worse than you want it to be, or is just so-so, you have three options, just like you would in a poker game: you can fold, you can bluff, or you can take action to make things better.

You can fold

It's easy to spot people who are not in the right job at a specific point in their career. No matter what they do to improve their work situation, they don't fit in. They know it, and everyone they work with knows it.

Perhaps your personal characteristics don't fit your job profile. Perhaps you've encountered negative circumstances in your job and are in a deep hole, unable to dig your way out. Perhaps you're simply not happy with your role. In situations like these, the best option may be to fold and move on to a new position.

Folding may be tough to do in the short term, yet in the long term, it could be the best decision you can make for your career. It's not my job as a coach to make sure you fit your role. It's my job as a coach to make sure you succeed. Sometimes you may find yourself in a situation where succeeding is just not likely to happen.

Take a moment to think about your current role and organization. What actions can you take to improve your work situation? Write your responses below. If you don't think any action will help, folding may be the best option for you.

_____

_____

_____

_____

_____

"You have three options: you can fold, you can bluff, or you can take action to **make things better**."

You can bluff

Bluffing is pretending to like something you don't like, whether it's an opinion, a feeling, an action, or a person. In poker, bluffing is a way to stay in the game with an inferior hand so you can ultimately win the jackpot.

Most of you have probably bluffed a feeling or delayed making a decision at some point in your career. Bluffing temporarily is sometimes the best thing to do. What I frequently find with my clients, however, is that they are bluffing for the long term. I have clients who don't like working for their boss, yet have been pretending for months (or years!) that they love their boss. Others have been avoiding a conversation they should have had long ago.

There are two drawbacks to bluffing for the long term. First, bluffing takes a lot of energy and creativity. As Walter Scott wrote in 1808, "Oh, what a tangled web we weave, / When first we practice to deceive!" Bluffing is hard and complicated, and at some point you'll make an error that will cause someone to observe or call your bluff. That will not help your career. Second, just like in a poker game, you may have to reveal your true hand at some point. As I tell my clients, it's usually better to be honest now than to be forced to be honest in the future.

Take a moment to think about things you are bluffing about in your organization or your career. Are you working on a project you hate? Are you working with someone who drives you crazy? In the space below, write down some actions or conversations you might be avoiding in the workplace. Are you ready to take action to improve them?

_____

_____

_____

_____

_____

You can take action to make things better

Whether your workplace poker hand inspires you to fold, bluff, or take action, you can be more successful in your career if you identify a few behaviors or actions that will better your situation.

This is not a complicated process. Spend some time thinking with yourself (see idea #2) to gain insight into the positive and not-so-positive aspects of your position. In the space below, write down at least one simple and realistic action you can take to make your workplace better.

_____

_____

_____

_____

_____

_____

The next time you go to work, think about how to make progress with this action. You can always start with a small step to ensure that progress happens.

WHEN TOMAS BEGINS to think about his workplace as a poker hand, he sees his potential promotion in a new light.

Whether he likes it or not, Tomas believes he doesn't have a good hand. The question is, what should he do about it? Should he fold and move to an engineering company with more integrity about its culture and work environment? Should he bluff, pretend things are better than they are, and get over it? Or should he take action to change what he can?

After chatting with some close colleagues and his coach, Tomas decides. He wants to be sure he has done everything he can to create the type of workplace that he'll enjoy and prosper in. He wants to take action! He accepts the promotion.

Although Tomas can't change everything in his workplace, he starts to identify small steps he can take to make positive progress. His first step? Work with his human resources business partner to make sure everyone is candid about the pluses and minuses of working at the firm.

WHAT'S NEXT FOR YOU?

If your company is not a great place to work, now is the time to take action rather than fold or bluff. What can you do differently today to ensure that you have better experiences in your workplace?

7

PAUSING
IS
POWERFUL

"It's not so much knowing when to speak, **when to pause**."

Jack Benny, comedian, vaudevillian, and actor

RAM'S EMPLOYEES REFER to him as a hard worker. If he could, he'd work twenty-five hours a day and do seventy-five things at the same time. He writes emails at all hours, calls colleagues from wherever he is, and sets aggressive deadlines for completing work. Ram is a high-energy work juggler.

To do all the work that Ram believes needs to be done, he moves fast. In his mind, the faster he moves, the more work he can do. He can't slow down because if he does, his competitors will catch up and pass him by. And he can't let that happen.

Unbeknownst to Ram, his peers and employees have a hard time keeping up with his fast pace. Even though his colleagues are all dedicated and loyal team members, few of them have Ram's energy or feel the need to work at all hours of the day. And while Ram thinks his energy level is invigorating and helpful, it doesn't naturally transfer well to others. Nor does he try to help others keep up with him.

Some of Ram's team members tolerate his behavior because he's the boss. Others, however, hate working for him. Many of Ram's colleagues are frustrated, feeling that if they can't keep up with him, they must be doing a poor job. Most of his team members love it when he leaves the office for a client meeting or a sales call, as they feel this is the only time they can focus on their work. A collective and exhaustive "Phew!" emanates from the office whenever Ram hops in his car and goes.

As time passes, Ram realizes that he's becoming increasingly disconnected from his staff. Morale is low. The team always takes too long to complete work that Ram feels is average at best. The direction that he gives seems to fall on deaf ears. Mistakes are larger and costlier than anticipated.

Is Ram somehow creating these situations? If so, can he do anything differently to raise morale, improve the quality of work, and feel more included in his team?

Yes. To be more effective as a leader, to better connect with his team members, and to drive his career forward, Ram—and you—should use the power of the pause.

Why is pausing so powerful?

Pausing does not necessarily mean working more slowly or taking a long time to decide or act. Pausing is a strategic activity that allows you to think more about your agenda, your workload, and your relationships before you interact with others or make decisions. Pausing is about thinking first and acting second.

"To be more effective as a leader, and to better connect with your team members, you should use the **power of the pause**."

By pausing and thinking first, you'll be able to manage your agenda more effectively, balance your workload better, and develop deeper working relationships with others. Showing people that you think before you decide will have a positive impact on how they perceive you.

Pausing will also help you avoid costly or time-consuming mistakes and will ultimately help you, your team, and your organization make more efficient progress. If you move too quickly in your interactions with colleagues, you will likely spend valuable time repeating things you've already explained, correcting errors that you or your colleagues have made, and apologizing to clients for mistakes that have occurred. Pausing will actually help you move faster.

Here's an example that occurred live, on global television, that illustrates how pausing could have prevented a major embarrassment and allowed an event to move faster.

At the 89th Academy Awards, in 2017, Warren Beatty and Faye Dunaway took the stage to present the Oscar for Best Picture. After they finished listing the nominees, Beatty opened the Oscar envelope and suddenly seemed confused. "And the Academy Award for Best Picture..." he began, looking uncomfortable as Dunaway encouraged him to keep going. "You're impossible," she teased him with an affectionate smile. "Come on," she urged.

Most viewers thought Beatty was joking to build tension, and after a few seconds (which felt like forever to those of us watching), he shook his head slightly and slipped the envelope to Dunaway. "*La La Land!*" she announced with glee. The audience went wild and the *La La Land* cast and crew ran onto the stage. Yet as the movie's producers began their emotional speeches, a stagehand interrupted the proceedings to say their movie had not in fact won the Best Picture Oscar. Beatty and Dunaway had been given the wrong envelope.

The *La La Land* producers handled the confusion as gracefully as they could, with one stepping back to the mic to announce that the actual winner was *Moonlight*. "This is not a joke," he said, and invited the producers, directors, and cast from that movie onto the stage. Before the *Moonlight* team accepted the award, Beatty returned to the mic and explained that the envelope he'd been given had contained the name of the Best Actress winner, Emma Stone, who starred in *La La Land*.

This confusion took up a lot of time and turned the event into a high-profile fiasco. Yet the gaffe could have been prevented if, after noticing something was wrong with the envelope, Beatty had paused for longer than he did. He could have said, "Ladies and gentlemen, we need to pause for a moment. I think I have the wrong envelope." The Academy Awards crew would have brought out the correct one, Beatty and Dunaway would have announced *Moonlight*, and the show would have gone on error-free.

Instead, Beatty quickly tried to figure out what to do with an award that didn't make sense to him, then, obviously feeling rushed by his co-presenter, thrust the envelope at her. Time was also wasted as we listened to the acceptance speeches from three *La La Land* producers; as that year's host, Jimmy Kimmel, tried to reconcile the parties; and as Beatty explained the error. If Beatty had paused to think as soon as he detected a mistake, the show would have ultimately moved faster and many people would not have experienced the deeply upsetting situation.

WHAT ABOUT YOU?

Do you work at a pace that's hard for others to keep up with? Can you think of any situations where your fast pace has led to a mistake, a redo, or the need to explain something again and again?

Why is it so hard to pause, and what are the downsides?

In today's business environment, many believe that if they're not moving fast and changing at an exponential rate, they risk becoming irrelevant. And many leaders, to avoid irrelevance, try to stay ahead of their competition by making decisions and acting quickly.

Most of my fast-moving clients, like Ram, are moving very, very fast. The idea of pausing sounds and feels contradictory to the concept of progress. You have to move fast to be the first to get to the future—don't you? The idea of pausing rarely enters my clients' minds.

Yet time and time again, when clients come to me for help with their careers and we look at their leadership style, we identify pace as a major concern.

Using the chart below, think about the pluses and minuses of working at an accelerated pace without ever stopping to pause. The pluses are the benefits to your career or your organization's growth. The minuses are detrimental to those things. I've filled in an example of each to get you started.

+   **−**

I feel in charge.   Employees' work is sloppy.

You will likely find that the pluses mostly reflect your own experiences while the minuses reflect the behavior of others. For example, your minuses may include observations like "People don't keep up with me," "I have to repeat things to people," "People do sloppy work," or "People are confused." Although you may think that solving these problems is about changing others' behaviors, many of them can be addressed by changing your pace. And the best way to change your pace is to use the power of the pause.

How can you add the power of the pause to your work life?

When I'm helping clients add the power of the pause to their work lives, I typically recommend two activities. While they may seem simple, the fact is that changing your behavior can be very hard to do. That's why we need two strategies.

Both of the following activities have the same goal: to help you remember to pause. One of the biggest challenges for anyone attempting to change a behavior is to *remember* to change. Once you remember to add the power of the pause to your decision-making process, you're much more likely to actually do it.

Create tactile reminders

Whether you're trying to build a better relationship with your boss, be more curious, or use the power of the pause, you need a reminder to practice the new behavior. A key strategy is to use a short-term tactile memory aid. I say "short-term" because you won't need to use the aid forever. Once your new behavior becomes a habit, you'll no longer need the reminder.

To help clients remember to change a behavior, I have found small colored stickers very effective. Yup. That's it. You can buy a package of a hundred stickers at an office

"Once you remember to add **the power of the pause** to your decision-making process, you're much more likely to actually do it."

supply store for a couple of dollars. Post a sticker on places where you look often during the day—on your laptop, your coffee cup, a whiteboard, or the inside of your office door—to remind you of the new behavior you want to adopt.

I like stickers because they're bright, cheap, and removable. You should feel free to use whatever tactile reminder works best for you.

Identify an accountability partner

It's hard to make changes by relying only on yourself. That's why I talked earlier about the value of an accountability partner (see idea #2). An accountability partner is a colleague who can help you, in the short term, modify an important behavior. An accountability partner proactively watches you and gives you instant feedback. They help you remember activities you need to do to make progress toward your desired change.

ONCE RAM BECOMES aware of the power of the pause, he works hard to adopt the new behavior. He doesn't operate slowly, because he does feel that an active pace is important. Yet after pausing more often to consider next steps, include his team, and give them clear direction, Ram begins to notice that the quality of work is going up, the number of mistakes is going down, and his relationship with his team is improving. By pausing more frequently, Ram is actually saving time in a very fast-paced world.

WHAT'S NEXT FOR YOU?

Practice pausing and you'll find you can actually move
more quickly. If you listen to others first and move forward
purposefully, you'll see better results for yourself and your
team.

IT'S ALL
ABOUT
FEEDBACK

"Feedback is
the bridge
to effectively
connect our
lesson-learned
from the past
to the future
**performance
and potential**."

Pearl Zhu, global corporate
executive and digital master

BUSAYO IS A supervisor in a medium-sized technology company. She has a very busy job, with almost a dozen technologists reporting to her. Some of her staff have been with the company for over ten years, and some for only a few weeks. Their industry knowledge, client service capabilities, and performance vary greatly.

The main feature of Busayo's leadership style—a feature she's proud of—is that she is a hands-off leader. She likes to tell her colleagues that her team members get their work done the way they want to get it done, and that she provides them with very little feedback. Busayo believes that giving feedback adds to an already busy workload and that she doesn't have time to do it. Plus, she gets no feedback from her boss either.

The only time Busayo provides feedback is when there's a client issue. If a client complains about the service they received from a technologist, Busayo is, as her team members put it, "all over you." Dealing with client criticism is not something she enjoys; it's the only time she loses her winning smile. What Busayo actually shares with her direct reports in these situations is not really feedback, but rather what she heard from the client and what she and the client want done to resolve the issue quickly. "Fix it and let's move on" is a common demand from Busayo.

Busayo is also poor at completing annual performance appraisals for her team. Most of her appraisals are delivered late, if at all. Some of her employees have gone years without one.

While some of Busayo's team members love her smile and easy way of leading, most feel that the lack of meaningful feedback from her—whether immediate or scheduled—makes her the worst boss they've ever had.

UNFORTUNATELY FOR BUSAYO'S team, and the company they all work for, Busayo is woefully unaware of the importance of providing feedback. And sadly, she is not alone.

Almost all of my clients are poor at giving immediate feedback, and many are poor at delivering scheduled performance appraisals. Interestingly, some people—including employees and managers—don't seem to care about this lack of feedback. You might think more organizations would manage with an iron fist and ensure, at least, that performance appraisals are completed as scheduled. Yet my experience with clients is that most people are working so quickly that they never think to pause to supply their direct reports with feedback.

Nevertheless, I say to my clients—and to you—that giving feedback is your most powerful leadership tool.

"Giving feedback is your most **powerful leadership tool**."

Why is giving feedback such a powerful leadership tool?

The goal of giving feedback is to guide employees to develop their own careers and to make sure the organization benefits as well.

Who better than a leader to share immediate feedback about something that could have been done better, or to supply scheduled feedback on an employee's overall performance and how it might evolve? Whether your employees have more or less experience than you, your feedback can lead them to think about the interactions they're having now and how they might handle those interactions more effectively in the future.

Delivering feedback is a win-win-win activity. Employees benefit by learning from their leader's insights and ideas, which helps them progress in their careers. Leaders benefit from the improved departmental performance that results from their employees moving in the right direction. And organizations benefit when feedback leads to improvements that save time, energy, and possibly money.

Feedback doesn't have to be delivered from the top down, from a supervisor to a direct report. Sharing feedback is also a valuable way for colleagues to help one another improve performance, work on problem areas, and become better drivers of their careers.

WHAT ABOUT YOU?

Do you give your team members immediate and scheduled feedback on a regular basis? If you don't, how might this behavior be hurting your team's performance and career development?

How can you provide feedback?

There are two types of feedback—immediate and scheduled—that will help you be a more powerful leader. The main differences between the two are shown in the table below.

Immediate	Scheduled
Brief	Overarching
Reactive yet future-focused	Proactive
Behavior-based	Performance-based

Immediate feedback typically has greater impact than scheduled feedback because it allows employees to modify their behavior in real time. That said, both types of feedback have benefits. When done well, they can complement each other.

Immediate feedback

The key characteristic of this type of feedback is in its name: it's immediate. Your goal is to provide this feedback while the behavior, including how others may have experienced it, is still fresh in your employee's mind. Feedback given within a few hours of the behavior typically qualifies as immediate.

The longer you wait to give this type of feedback, the less impact it will have. Imagine talking about a roller coaster ride immediately after the ride is over as opposed to talking about it two weeks later. Immediately after the ride, the rush is still with you. You're more likely to see and feel your experience. "Woo-hoo! Wow! What a ride!" Two weeks later? You might not remember what the ride felt like at all.

Immediate feedback can be positive, to let an individual know that something they just did was effective and had a good impact, or it can be constructive, to say that something they just did was not effective or less effective than it could be. Positive feedback reinforces a particularly good behavior. Constructive feedback helps an employee think about managing their behavior differently in the future.

Three characteristics of immediate feedback help this type of communication really stand out. Immediate feedback is:

- **Brief.** No one will welcome a thirty-minute lecture on how they could have done something differently. Most people don't have a lot of time to receive, or provide, long-winded feedback. Typically, two to seven minutes is enough. Sometimes you can give meaningful feedback with a few words that take only a moment to say.

- **Reactive yet future-focused.** You are providing insights and observations *after* the employee's behavior has occurred. While this may feel like a negative—nobody likes to be reactive—it's actually a fantastic way to help your direct report experience, in the moment, how they can manage their behavior in the future. Hearing feedback right after the event occurs will help the receiver digest it better.

- **Behavior-based.** Since this type of feedback is immediate, brief, and reactive, your focus should be on your employee's behavior. *Merriam-Webster* defines behavior as "the way in which someone conducts oneself." Your goal is to make your employees more aware of how their conduct affects others and to encourage them to behave in ways that are better for everyone.

There are two types of immediate feedback you can provide: pre-identified and random.

1. **Pre-identified immediate feedback.** This is feedback given at the recipient's request to help that person modify a behavior they've received constructive feedback about before. The topic of the feedback depends on the individual, but it should focus on the behavior the individual has demonstrated and wants to change.

   For example, a colleague may ask you one day, "Would be willing to give me feedback on something? I've been told that I doodle and play with my hands a lot during meetings, which is distracting for some people. I've been working hard to stay focused on the speaker so that I don't do this as much. Could you watch me during the meeting and let me know right afterward what you saw?" Any feedback you give this colleague from now on would fall into the category of pre-identified immediate feedback.

2. **Random immediate feedback.** This is feedback given any time you notice behavior that you think is important for an employee or colleague to be aware of. You might approach an employee one day and say, "I happened to notice a couple of things in our meeting a few moments ago that I'd like to share some feedback on. Are you open to hearing this feedback?"

In both scenarios, permission is requested to observe or offer feedback, and the conversation occurs immediately after the event at which the behavior happens.

Scheduled feedback

Scheduled feedback is delivered as part of a regular process such as an annual performance appraisal. There are many regular feedback processes in the corporate world. Typically they involve a specific timetable, pre-established forms, and identified delivery methods. Although the content may vary, the processes themselves tend to be very structured.

I could write a book on the topic of annual performance appraisals—opinions on their effectiveness vary dramatically. Some people find them very effective. Performance appraisals seem most beneficial in newer organizations where more structure is needed to ensure progress. Other people find performance appraisals overly structured. This opinion tends to be strongest within large organizations that want more flexibility, or that have tried a structured process and are ready to move on to a less structured one.

In reality, most organizations either don't have a scheduled feedback process or they have one that is creakily implemented.

If you're a leader in an organization that uses scheduled feedback, you have an obligation to implement the process well, even if others around you don't. Done well, scheduled feedback is an opportunity to have a meaningful conversation with your employees. That's because it is:

- **Overarching.** One of the beauties of an annual appraisal is that it gives you a place to recap, in detail, the successes and failures of the prior year and discuss what the employee should work on in the coming year. You can give your employee big-picture direction on how they should spend their time and energy. The ability to have a longer conversation and offer deeper observations and recommendations is the hallmark of a successful appraisal.

- **Proactive.** Scheduled feedback allows you to sit down with your employee and proactively discuss their career direction along with their performance, projects, and deliverables. An appraisal conversation is an opportunity to find out how your employee is doing in their current role, what their next role might be, and how you can help get them get there. You can look ahead this way because a scheduled conversation is longer and more future-focused than an immediate feedback session.

- **Performance-based.** A scheduled appraisal is your chance to give your employee performance-based rather than behavior-based feedback. Performance-based feedback is more long term and directional than the behavior-based variety. It looks at the next two to three years and considers broader career direction. Behavior-based feedback, on the other hand, is short term and impactful in the moment it's happening, which is why it's the basis of immediate feedback.

What if I'm not getting feedback?

"I am this person! I haven't had formal performance assessments or meaningful feedback for years!" That's what I hear from many of my clients who work in organizations that aren't serious about providing feedback.

Unfortunately, this is part of the poker hand these clients have been dealt (see idea #6). It may be part of your poker hand too. Remember that with any hand, you have three options: fold, bluff, or take action. However, when it comes to feedback, you should choose the last option. Your career is too important to fly blind (or drive blindfolded).

The simplest action you can take to get feedback—positive or negative—is to ask your boss for it. You can also be proactive and write a self-appraisal of what you've done well over the past year and what you want to do differently to get a different outcome. You can share this document with your boss and ask for comments. After all, it's better to have something in your employee file about your accomplishments and areas of opportunity than nothing at all.

FORTUNATELY FOR BUSAYO and her team, Busayo eventually learns about the importance of feedback.

Wanting to experience a win-win-win for herself, her staff, and her company, she starts to look for opportunities to provide immediate feedback to her team. She asks each of her direct reports if she can suggest one or two behavioral changes that will help them be more effective. Everyone says yes. Now Busayo has a new way to engage with her employees and influence their work style. Busayo also meets with her human resources business partner to create a roadmap for conducting scheduled feedback. (A career driver always welcomes a map!) Now Busayo has a regular and effective way to share successes and influence her team's performance.

The result is the triple win Busayo is looking for. Her employees win by getting both immediate and scheduled feedback on how to behave and perform in their workplace. Busayo wins by making an immediate and lasting positive impact on the performance and growth of her department and her subordinates. And the company wins because everyone does their job better and contributes to the evolution of the organization as a whole.

"The simplest action you can take to get feedback—positive or negative—is to **ask your boss for it**."

WHAT'S NEXT FOR YOU?

If you are giving your team members immediate and scheduled feedback, could you make this feedback even better? If you're not doing this and you want to begin, what are the first steps you can take?

9

ACTUALLY, IT'S ALL ABOUT EMPATHY

"**When you show deep empathy** toward others, their defensive energy goes down, and positive energy replaces it."

Stephen Covey, educator, author, and businessperson

JAVIER WORKS AS a corporate development officer for a large nonprofit in Boston. His job is to raise his organization's visibility in the business community for the purpose of fundraising. It's a competitive market out there for raising funds, and Javier thinks he and his team do a very good job. In the decade Javier has been on the job, he and his team have met or exceeded their fundraising goal each and every year.

Despite this, Javier has a terrible relationship with his CEO, Jim, who has led the nonprofit for two years. Javier, who is one of my clients, told me one day, "If Jim and I are walking down a hallway toward each other, I will go into an office or turn down another hallway just to avoid connecting with him." Javier avoids meeting with Jim as much as possible, and when they do meet, it's almost always at Jim's request. Javier perceives Jim as a "long talker" and hates speaking with him. "A simple 'good morning' to Jim," he says, "can easily turn into a thirty-minute conversation that I don't have time for."

Even worse, Javier feels that Jim gives him no credit for the work he and his team are doing. Instead, Jim deluges Javier with ideas and suggestions that he believes can make next year's fundraising results even better. "He says things like, 'Last year was last year. Listen to these ideas I thought of for next year!'" Javier tells me. "It's so demoralizing."

Javier has gone from being an engaged and optimistic employee in the first eight years at his organization to a defensive and negative employee in the last two years. How did this happen?

As part of my coaching engagement with Javier, I had a chance to meet with Jim about his expectations. Our conversation clarified for me why Javier has such an issue with Jim. Not only did I confirm that Jim is indeed a long talker, but everything he has to say is about himself: *his* thoughts, *his* ideas, *his* experiences. Rarely in our discussion did he refer to a colleague or a colleague's situation unless he was talking about his relationship with or expectations for that person. In a nutshell, Jim completely lacks empathy.

What is empathy and why does it matter?

If you google the word "empathy," here's one definition that will pop up:

em·pa·thy noun
the ability to understand and share the feelings of another

synonyms: affinity with, rapport with, sympathy with, understanding of, sensitivity toward, sensibility to, identification with, awareness of, fellowship with, fellow feeling for, like-mindedness, togetherness, closeness to

In Jim's daily behavior with his colleagues, he fails to demonstrate any of the key words associated with empathy. That's why Javier, and others who report to Jim, don't like working for him. That's why Javier doesn't feel valued or respected by Jim. That's why Jim doesn't engage with any of Javier's ideas but keeps pushing his own views as if Javier's don't matter. Jim's apparent lack of empathy has a huge effect on how others experience him in the workplace.

If you don't regularly demonstrate empathy, your colleagues will feel like you don't understand or care about them. They won't feel connected to you or what you are doing. Defensive and negative energy will build, and responsive and positive energy will dissipate. A lack of empathy will make you seem cold to, and disconnected from, others.

On the other hand, if you demonstrate empathy often, your colleagues will feel more connected to you. You'll be seen as warm and caring rather than cold and disconnected. If you're the leader, people will bring problems to your attention earlier and more often. Because they believe you care about what they have to say, colleagues will chat with you more about what's going on in the office. Folks will be more positively engaged and energized in your workplace.

People want to work with people who they believe care about them as an individual. Demonstrating empathy is a win-win-win situation—you benefit and so do the others around you, and the organization becomes a better place to work.

WHAT ABOUT YOU?

Have you mastered the ability to show empathy toward others in your workplace? If you don't demonstrate empathy, how might this be negatively affecting your team?

What does empathy look like?

Let's look at an example. Imagine that Javier's mother is very ill. Javier is an only child, and his father passed away five years ago. Javier devotes a lot of time and energy to caring for his sick mother, and this is interfering with his focus and commitment at work.

Here are two conversations that might occur between Javier and Jim, one in which Jim does not demonstrate empathy and one in which he's highly empathetic.

SCENARIO 1

JAVIER: Thanks for having this meeting today, Jim. I appreciate hearing your ideas for fundraising next year. I also wanted to share an idea that my team and I have been working on.

JIM: I've got to move to my next meeting, Javier. Can you tell it to me quickly?

"Demonstrating empathy is a win-win situation—you benefit and so do the **others around you**."

JAVIER: I don't know if I can abbreviate the topic, Jim. I'd really like at least half an hour to chat with you about it.

JIM: We're awfully busy here, Javier. If it's that complicated, maybe you should work on it next year. Focusing on ideas we currently have in place, and the ideas I just shared with you, might make you and your team more productive. You're missing a lot of deadlines.

JAVIER: Sorry, but I've been dealing with some problems at home.

JIM: We need to leave home stuff at home, Javier. When you're at work, you need to be more productive.

JAVIER: I actually think we've been very productive. We've met or even exceeded our fundraising goals for each of the last ten years.

JIM: Your fundraising goals are another point of discussion. I think they've been set too low. How do you generate your annual fundraising goals?

JAVIER: I think we're getting off topic. I'm not ready to have this type of conversation today. I'm having a really hard time at home.

JIM: Look, we're out of time, Javier. I've got to get to my next meeting. Tell me about it next week.

If we go back to the earlier definition of empathy, which of the following do you feel Jim demonstrated during this brief conversation?

- ☐ affinity
- ☐ rapport
- ☐ sympathy
- ☐ understanding
- ☐ sensitivity
- ☐ sensibility
- ☐ identification
- ☐ awareness
- ☐ fellowship
- ☐ fellow feeling
- ☐ like-mindedness
- ☐ togetherness
- ☐ closeness

Now let's imagine a different kind of conversation.

SCENARIO 2

JIM: Hey, Javier. I was wondering if you had a couple of minutes to chat with me today.

JAVIER: Uh. Sure, Jim. Is everything okay?

JIM: Well, I've noticed over the past few days that something seems to be troubling you, and I'd like to chat with you about it. Do you have a few minutes now?

JAVIER: Sure. Can we chat about it in your office?

[THEY GO INTO JIM'S OFFICE.]

JIM: I saw that you missed some deadlines recently, which is not normal for you. Is everything okay?

JAVIER: Thanks for asking. I know I haven't been myself lately. I'm sorry about that. It's my mom. I'm an only child and my dad died a few years ago. My mom is really ill now, and taking care of her is exhausting.

JIM: I'm sorry to hear that, Javier. She's lucky to have you. I haven't experienced any elder care issues myself. This must be very tough for you. Is there anything I can do to help?

JAVIER: To be honest, the more I can focus on work, the better I'll navigate this tough time. I have a fundraising idea I would love to share with you. Do you have time tomorrow morning to chat about it?

JIM: Sounds great. I'd love to help. Let's meet tomorrow at nine.

If we go back to the definition of empathy, which of the following do you feel Jim demonstrated in this conversation?

☐ affinity
☐ rapport
☐ sympathy
☐ understanding
☐ sensitivity
☐ sensibility
☐ identification
☐ awareness
☐ fellowship
☐ fellow feeling
☐ like-mindedness

☐ togetherness
☐ closeness

Chances are, you checked more boxes this time. Jim demonstrated deep empathy in the conversation with Javier. By showing that he heard and understood Javier's feelings, Jim shared a positive, energy-building interaction with him. And Jim's openness to hearing Javier's idea might lead to a strategy that's highly successful for the organization.

In scenario 1—the scenario that, unfortunately, would most likely play out during a conversation between my client and his boss—Jim demonstrated very little empathy, leaving Javier feeling defensive and de-energized. Jim will never help his organization generate creative new ideas or evolve if he continues to lack empathy.

How can you demonstrate empathy?

Most of the clients I work with want to be more empathetic; they just don't know how to do it. Empathy is something we seldom learn in school or in the workplace, even though it's so important. While some people think empathy is something you either have or don't have, I believe that any behavior can improve with practice. Whether you're born with it or not, you need to show appropriate empathy to be effective as a leader or to steer your way forward at any stage of your career.

Scenario 2 between Jim and Javier illustrates six key steps for demonstrating empathy.

"You need to show empathy to **be effective as a leader** or to steer your way forward at any stage of your career."

1: Notice the behaviors of others

Sometimes your colleagues are upbeat and focused, and sometimes they're offbeat and unfocused. To demonstrate empathy, you need to see the differences. If you don't know how to notice the behavior of others, or don't like to do it, you should work on improving this skill.

Begin by picking one person you work with and discreetly observing their behavior over the course of a week. See if you can identify any positive or negative shifts in their mood. Once you start to see the differences we all experience, you'll be making progress.

In scenario 2, where Jim demonstrated empathy, he noticed that Javier wasn't behaving as usual and that something might be bothering him. While a colleague might in some cases approach you to say they're having a tough day, your ability to notice that person's behavior on your own is an important skill.

2: Ask permission to speak with your colleague

Asking permission to speak with a person is a key step in any relationship when you need to discuss a potentially difficult topic. Asking permission is easy. As you saw in scenario 2, Jim simply asked Javier if he had a few minutes to chat.

3: Be clear about why you want to speak with your colleague

If you're not clear about what you want to discuss, you may end up confusing your colleague and making their situation worse. Jim was direct in saying that he'd noticed Javier had missed some deadlines recently and that this was unusual for him. That's a terrific example of being clear.

4: Ask your colleague if you can do anything to help

Be direct about your concern and your ability to help, as your colleague may be uncomfortable or unable to talk about whatever is affecting them. Offer your colleague a place where they can get their concern out on the table. The more you know about the issue, the better equipped you'll be to assess whether you can help. Simply asking if you can help, as Jim did in scenario 2, is a key component of demonstrating empathy. Your colleague may not need your help, but it's important to offer it.

5: Acknowledge your colleague's feelings

Most people want others to listen to their story, even if the listener is not an expert on the topic or can't help solve the problem. Make sure you acknowledge the situation your colleague is experiencing and the impact it's having on them. As you saw in scenario 2, after hearing Javier's story about his mother, Jim said that the situation sounded tough.

6: Reiterate to your colleague that you're there to help

You want to leave the conversation on a high note, so at the end, reiterate your acknowledgment of whatever is troubling your colleague and your interest in helping as best as you can. This will make your colleague feel listened to and supported. Follow up with your colleague within a week or so to confirm they're making progress with their issue. This shows that you listened to them and that you care.

Put these six steps together and you get empathy! Here's a recap so you can begin to practice the steps as soon as the next opportunity arises:

1. Notice behavior
2. Ask permission to speak
3. Be clear
4. Offer to help
5. Acknowledge feelings
6. Reiterate your offer to help

IMAGINE JIM'S IMPACT as a leader of the nonprofit if he were a role model of empathy. He would be known as a good listener and a leader who cares. He would put the team's needs first by noticing their behavior and showing his curiosity. His colleagues would feel more engaged and energized at work. Folks would feel they had a terrific relationship with Jim and would work harder for him. The organization would be a great place to show up every day. Who wouldn't want that?

Javier decides that since he can't influence Jim's behavior directly, he can try to do it through role-modeling. Javier shows empathy to others in the workplace whenever he can, and his colleagues feel increasingly comfortable coming to him with concerns and issues. Javier hopes that in time, Jim will notice this behavior and begin to adopt it for himself.

WHAT'S NEXT FOR YOU?

If you are known for being empathetic, how can you teach others to show empathy more often? If you seldom show empathy, how can you use the suggestions in this chapter to start practicing empathy with others?

CONCLUSION

NO ONE IS perfect. Each one of us, at work and in life, does some things really well and other things not so well. My intent, with the ideas in this book, is not to make you perfect. It's to make you more aware of what you can do to shift from the passenger's seat of your career to the driver's seat. You are in charge of you.

We can all get better at developing our strengths and addressing our weaknesses. Even great leaders can change their behavior and become better leaders in the process. Whatever your situation is, you can do things differently tomorrow than you did today. Once you accept that, and practice it, you'll be able to steer your career in the direction you want it to go, earn the respect of your colleagues, and be more productive and happier at work.

Where will you start? Take a moment to write down the top three behaviors and actions you want to start practicing:

I _____

2 _____

3 _____

Find a trusted colleague, an accountability partner, an accountability team, or a coach to help you look for ways to bring these behaviors to life.

As I've learned from my clients over the past twelve years, everyone can adopt one or two—or five—of the ideas in this book and see improvement. You don't have to apply them all. You just need to apply enough to make progress.

As a former boss of mine at Iron Mountain used to say, "Progress is better than perfection." When it comes to driving your career forward, I couldn't agree more.

"Progress is better than perfection."

ACKNOWLEDGMENTS

LET'S FACE IT—WRITING a book is a solo experience. While the ideas may come from your experiences with others, the activity of writing takes place early in the morning, late in the evening, or sitting at a corner table at your local café. That said, a number of people have played a spiritual role in helping me put these thoughts into print and I would like to thank them now.

My wife, Kathy, is the funniest, smartest, and sexiest person I have ever met. She has improved my life significantly; and secretly, my writings are an offshoot of my desire to make sure she has the best life possible.

I am inspired daily by the evolution of my two daughters, Caroline and Sara. Kathy and I call it "adulting"—the ongoing effort of transition from childhood to adulthood. "Dad, I just got an insurance bill for my new car. What do I do?" asks my daughter Caroline. "Welcome to adulthood, honey. Let's chat about how you can pay for it." We are loving every minute of it.

As I'm self-employed, my conversations with myself are what Kathy calls a "staff meeting." While I don't have a staff, three key colleagues—Karen Burke, Dan Fisher, and Sarah Mann—keep me inspired to make the world a better place.

In 2017, when the ideas in this book came to fruition, I was reading *The Coaching Habit: Say Less, Ask More & Change the Way You Lead Forever*, by Michael Bungay Stanier. He also blogged about how a company called Page Two played a huge role in the success of his book.

I won't go into detail here, yet the publication of my first book, *Raise Your Visibility & Value: Uncover the Lost Art of Connecting on the Job*, was met with a series of unexpected challenges. I needed a new publishing experience, so I reached out to Page Two and ultimately hired this organization to help me bring this book to you. I want to thank Chris Brandt, Taysia Louie, Gabrielle Narsted, Lana Okerlund, Frances Peck, Alison Strobel, Lorraine Toor, and Trena White of Page Two for their dedicated assistance, unfiltered candor, attention to detail, and recurring support. I could not have completed this book without them.

ENDNOTES

1. Gallup, *State of the American Manager: Analytics and Advice for Leaders*, 2015, https://www.gallup.com/services/182138/state-american-manager.aspx.

2. Richard Rumelt, *Good Strategy/Bad Strategy: The Difference and Why It Matters* (New York: Crown Business, 2011), 239.

3. Grace Ferguson, "Why Are Long-Term Employees Important?" *Chron*, accessed November 4, 2019, https://smallbusiness.chron.com/longterm-employees-important-40711.html.

ABOUT
THE AUTHOR

ED EVARTS is the founder and president of Excellius Leadership Development, a Boston-based coaching organization. He works with successful leaders to increase their self-awareness so they can manage themselves more productively; with successful teams to ensure their time together is as productive as possible; and with smaller organizations, at a pivot point in their evolution, to help them plan strategically and purposefully.

Ed is the author of *Raise Your Visibility & Value: Uncover the Lost Art of Connecting on the Job* and the host of *Be Brave @ Work*, a weekly podcast in which leaders share stories about bravery—or the lack of it—in their careers, and the impact their choices have had on their career progression.

Ed is a past president of the International Coach Federation of New England, the fifth-largest coaching affiliation group in the United States.

You can reach Ed at one of the following:
ed@excellius.com
617-549-1391
www.excellius.com